BRIGHT IDEA BOOKS

KOMODO
Dragons

by Maddie Spalding

Content Consultant

Luke Welton
Collection Manager
Biodiversity Institute & Natural History Museum
University of Kansas

CAPSTONE PRESS
a capstone imprint

Bright Idea Books are published by Capstone Press
1710 Roe Crest Drive, North Mankato, Minnesota 56003
www.mycapstone.com

Library of Congress Cataloging-in-Publication Data
Names: Spalding, Maddie, 1990- author.
Title: Komodo dragons / by Maddie Spalding.
Description: North Mankato, Minnesota : Capstone Press, [2020] | Series:
    Unique animal adaptations | Audience: Grade 4 to 6. | Includes
    bibliographical references and index.
Identifiers: LCCN 2018061083 (print) | LCCN 2018061649 (ebook) | ISBN
    9781543571738 (ebook) | ISBN 9781543571530 (hardcover) | ISBN 9781543575071 (paperback)
Subjects: LCSH: Komodo dragon--Juvenile literature. | Komodo
    dragon--Adaptation--Juvenile literature.
Classification: LCC QL666.L29 (ebook) | LCC QL666.L29 S68 2020 (print) | DDC 597.95/968--dc23
LC record available at https://lccn.loc.gov/2018061083

All internet sites appearing in back matter were available and accurate when this book was sent
to press.

Editorial Credits
Editor: Marie Pearson
Designer: Becky Daum
Production Specialist: Colleen McLaren

Photo Credits
iStockphoto: funky-data, 25, MikeLane45, 19; Shutterstock Images: Daniel Karfik, 20–21, Don
Mammoser, 9, Erni, 5, Gudkov Andrey, cover, 22–23, 28, Kiwisoul, 12–13, Kjersti Joergensen,
14–15, Rafal Cichawa, 6–7, Richard Susanto, 26–27, Sergey Uryadnikov, 10–11, 16, Viktor Loki,
30–31

Design Elements: Shutterstock Images

TABLE OF CONTENTS

CHAPTER 1

ON THE
Hunt

A giant lizard flicks its tongue. It creeps through the open forest. This huge lizard is the Komodo dragon. Komodo dragons are the world's largest lizards. They are about 10 feet (3 meters) long. They can weigh more than 300 pounds (140 kilograms). Males grow bigger than females.

A Komodo dragon is a large, powerful lizard.

Wild Komodo dragons live only on islands in Indonesia. They are named after one of the islands: Komodo.

The lizard has brown scales. It has strong muscles. Its claws are powerful.

6

Komodo Island has beaches and hills.

GOOD SWIMMERS

Komodos are great swimmers. They sometimes swim from one island to another.

CHAPTER 2

ADAPTATIONS and Other Features

All animals have **adaptations**. These can be skills. They can be body parts. They help animals survive.

Komodo dragons are **reptiles**. Their bodies cannot control their temperature. They may use sunlight to stay warm. They may find shade to cool off.

Nights are often chilly. The lizards have sharp claws. They dig **burrows**. Burrows help them stay warm.

Burrows stay warmer than the open air at night.

9

Komodos have scales. The scales are like armor. They protect the lizards from attacks. Sometimes Komodos fight each other. They use their claws to defend themselves. Claws also help them dig and climb trees.

A Komodo's tail is strong. The tail helps the lizard glide through water. A Komodo also uses its tail to stand up. It stands up to fight other Komodos.

Komodos' tough scales keep them safe during fights.

HUNTING

The Komodo has hunting skills. It cannot see or hear well. But it has a special **organ** in its mouth. The organ is the Jacobson's organ. It helps the lizard smell.

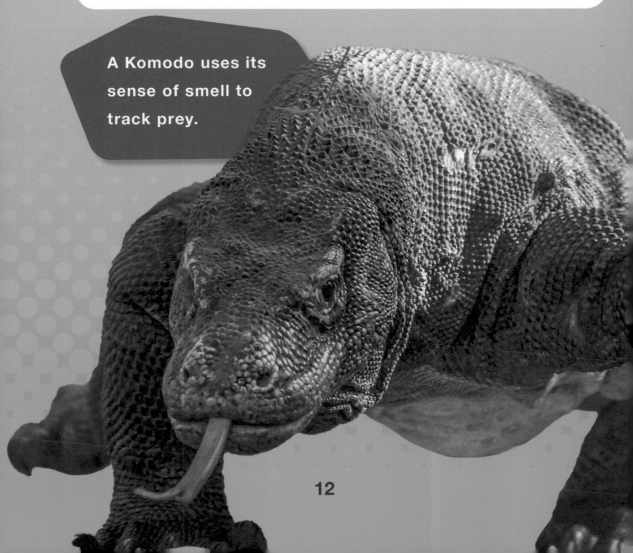

A Komodo uses its sense of smell to track prey.

The lizard's tongue collects scents in the air. It brings the scents to the organ. The organ tells the lizard when **prey** is near. A Komodo's tongue is forked. The scent may be stronger on one side of the tongue. This tells the lizard where a smell comes from. It can smell dead animals up to 2.5 miles (4 kilometers) away.

JACOBSON'S ORGAN

Most lizards and snakes have a Jacobson's organ. So do some mammals.

Komodos follow the scent of prey. Their main prey is deer. When the lizards get close to prey, they chase it. The lizards can run up to 13 miles (21 km) per hour. Their jaws are strong. They latch onto prey.

Komodos can take down large prey, including deer.

15

A Komodo's teeth are sharp. It sinks its teeth into prey. **Glands** in its jaws release **venom**. It mixes with saliva. The mixture oozes into an animal's wound. It thins the animal's blood. This makes the animal bleed easily. Some prey escape, but they do not live long.

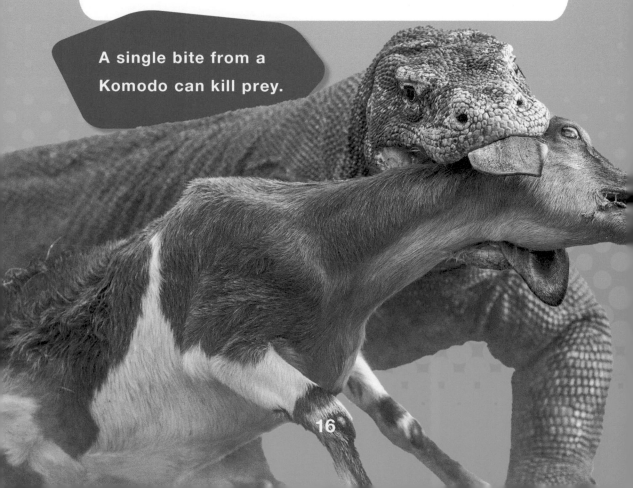

A single bite from a Komodo can kill prey.

A Komodo can eat big meals. Its stomach stretches. This lets the lizard eat large prey. It **digests** food slowly. The lizard soaks in sunlight. Heat speeds up digestion. Komodos can go weeks without eating.

TOO FULL TO MOVE

A Komodo can eat up to 80 percent of its body weight. This extra weight makes it hard to move. The lizard throws up its meal when threatened. This helps it run from danger.

CHAPTER 3

LIFE
Cycle

A female Komodo digs many holes. Most are fake nests. Only one will hold her eggs. She lays about 30 eggs in the nest. She guards them. Other Komodos try to eat the eggs. They have to search all the holes for the eggs. The female has tricked the **predators**.

Fake nests
can keep other
Komodos from
finding the
real one.

GROWING UP

Life for young Komodos is dangerous. They have predators. Even adult Komodos try to eat them! Young lizards stay safe by climbing trees. Adults cannot climb trees. They are too heavy.

Young Komodos find food in trees. They eat small lizards and insects. They eat snakes and birds too.

Young Komodos are good climbers.

Komodos can live up to 30 years. Adults eat almost any food they find. As adults, their only predator is other Komodos.

Adult Komodos only need to protect themselves against other adults.

CHAPTER 4

PROTECTING Komodo Dragons

Komodo dragons once lived in all of Indonesia. They also lived in Australia. Today they live only on five islands. About 6,000 Komodos live there. Some land they live on is protected. It is called Komodo National Park.

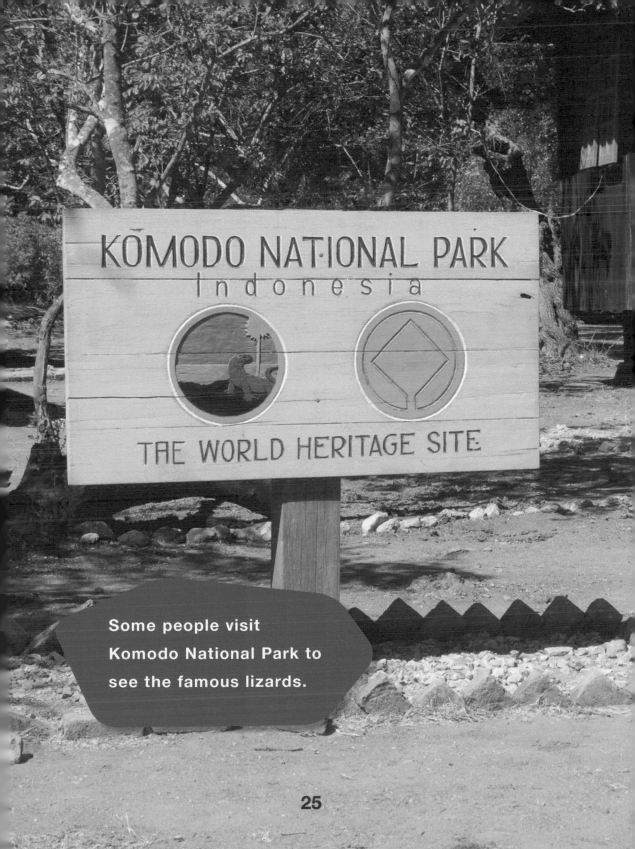

Some people visit Komodo National Park to see the famous lizards.

Komodos face threats. Humans on Flores Island hunt deer. So there are fewer deer for the Komodos to eat. Scientists try to solve this problem. They work with villagers. They help protect Komodo dragons. Many people want these giant lizards to live on.

Many people are working to save Komodos.

GLOSSARY

adaptation
a behavior or body part that helps an animal survive in its environment

burrow
a hole in the ground where animals sleep

digest
to break down food so that it can be used by the body

gland
a part of the body that produces a substance

organ
a part of the body that has a specific purpose

predator
an animal that eats other animals

prey
an animal that is hunted by another animal

reptile
an animal that breathes air, has a backbone, and uses the environment to control its body temperature; most reptiles lay eggs and have scaly skin

venom
a toxic substance an animal's body produces that is injected into prey or predators

TRIVIA

1. A Komodo dragon swings its head from side to side to smell food from different directions.

2. A Komodo dragon's saliva contains about 50 different kinds of bacteria.

3. In 2009, scientists found fossils in Australia. They were approximately 300,000 to 4 million years old. They appeared to have come from ancient Komodo dragons.

4. In 1990, the president of Indonesia gave U.S. President George H.W. Bush a Komodo dragon as a gift. Bush donated the lizard to the Cincinnati Zoo.

ACTIVITY

VENOMOUS REPTILES

Komodo dragons are not the only reptiles that release venom. Some snakes and lizards use venom to defend themselves or kill prey. Choose one of the following animals to learn about:

- Gila monster
- cobra
- iguana
- rattlesnake

Look online to find information about this animal. Create a poster to teach people about the animal. Is the animal's venom strong? How does the animal use its venom?

FURTHER RESOURCES

Curious about cool reptiles? Check out these resources:

DKfindout! Monitor Lizards
https://www.dkfindout.com/us/animals-and-nature/reptiles/monitor-lizards/

Ringstad, Arnold. *Totally Amazing Facts about Reptiles*. Mind Benders. North Mankato, Minn.: Capstone Publishing, 2018.

Sherman, Jill. *Komodo Dragons*. Real-Life Dragons. North Mankato, Minn.: Capstone Publishing, 2017.

Want to know more about animal adaptations? Learn more here:

Amstutz, Lisa J. *Thorny Devil Lizards and Other Extreme Reptile Adaptations*. Extreme Adaptations. North Mankato, Minn.: Capstone Publishing, 2015.

PBS Nature Works: Structural and Behavioral Adaptations
https://nhpbs.org/natureworks/nwep1.htm

INDEX